John Fentress Gardner

Melville's Vision of America

A New Interpretation of Moby Dick

Proceedings
Number 32
The Myrin Institute

The Myrin Institute, Inc.
for Adult Education
521 Park Avenue
New York, New York 10021

University Address
Waldorf School
Adelphi University
Garden City, New York 11530

Proceedings is published periodically as a reflection of the Myrin Institute's purpose and activities. The Institute believes that a genuine reconciliation of the modern scientific attitude with a spiritual world-concept is the most essential need of modern man.

Table of Contents

Proceedings Number 32

Library of Congress Catalogue Card No. 77-80051
ISBN 0-913098-07-8

Akin to the adventure of Perseus and Andromeda—indeed, by some supposed to be indirectly derived from it—is that famous story of St. George and the Dragon; which dragon I maintain to have been a whale; for in many old chronicles whales and dragons are strangely jumbled together, and often stand for each other. "Thou art as a lion of the waters, and as a dragon of the sea," saith Ezekiel; hereby plainly meaning a whale; in truth, some versions of the Bible use that word itself. Besides, it would much subtract from the glory of the exploit had St. George but encountered a crawling reptile of the land, instead of doing battle with the great monster of the deep. Any man may kill a snake, but only a Perseus, a St. George . . . have the heart in them to march boldly up to a whale.

"The Honor and Glory of Whaling,"
Moby Dick

Illustration by Elizabeth deJong

Foreword

John Fentress Gardner's unique interpretation of *Moby Dick* is the result of a forty-year study and seventeen years of classroom teaching. He taught Melville, Whitman and Emerson in an American literature course for high school seniors in the Waldorf School, Garden City, New York.* The course became a mind- and heart-opener for many of them, and for the parents and teachers who were able to attend from time to time.

Nevertheless, it was not until 1976 that John Gardner felt ready to write a chapter on Melville for a book he hopes to complete under the title, *Heralds of the American Spirit.* By a happy destiny, therefore, this present article was finished in the summer of America's bicentennial year.

Melville, Emerson and Whitman, along with Thoreau, were the prophets and shapers of American culture. In an earlier *Proceedings,* "The Idea of Man in America," Dr. Gardner presented their views on the nature of man. The following article pictures, through Melville's visionary eyes, America's future task. *Moby Dick*, it will be seen, is indeed a prophecy, one that goes to the heart of our present condition.

Every great myth moves us at various times with special force and poignancy. With John Gardner's help, Melville's epic of the great white whale can become as significant to Americans now as

* Dr. Gardner was Faculty Chairman of this school for twenty-five years. He now directs Adelphi University's Waldorf Institute for Liberal Education, a graduate program in teacher education, in addition to his activities as Chairman of the Myrin Institute. He is also founder of the Council for Educational Freedom in America.

Perseus was to the Greeks, Ezekiel to the Hebrews, and St. George to the British. It is time we marched boldly up to this whale.

> Moby Dick *was prophetic in showing that times were coming when men must once again reckon with the supernatural. The battle of good against evil is becoming ever more explicit; and those who wish to fight on the side of the good must want, and seek, and learn to receive, help—in a modern way—from the living spirit of goodness. To use the appropriate mythic analogy, those who would fight Leviathan, the dragon power, should pray for inspiration and courage from Marduk-Michael, wielder of the sacred sword and spear.*
> "Melville's Vision of America"

Herman Melville

"We hear that Melville married, had children, and lived by bread obscurely, like other men; so whence came this star dust, unearthly bright with original energy after so many years, that is scattered throughout his work, lighting up spectral meanings in common words?"
—H.M. Tomlinson

Melville's Vision of America

"I see a whale in the South-sea drinking my soul away."
William Blake, in *America*, 1793

Moby Dick is said to be the most intensively studied book in American literature. Though it sold few copies and was scornfully treated by many of the critics who bothered to take notice of it when it first appeared in 1851, it began to come into its own in the 1920s. Since then, it has received numerous scholarly interpretations, been assigned to countless English classes in high school and college, and become generally recognized as a major work that has something of great importance to say about the condition of the modern soul. Many readers, indeed, have had the feeling that the tragedy of the *Pequod* under Captain Ahab is in some way prophetic for American society and the American ship of state.

My own acquaintance with *Moby Dick* came at the age of about nineteen. I was captivated equally by its strength and by its beauty. It was for me full of portents and presentiments, expressed in language of extraordinary power. I did not get far in trying to lift the mystical truths I sensed on every page out of the language in which they were embedded, so I left them in it, simply reading and rereading many passages as they stood, until I had virtually memorized them. I delighted in the alliterative music of Melville's words, and in the surging flow of his sentences. His was indeed "a bold and nervous lofty language"! And its strange hints about the wonders and vicissitudes of human life were of fascinating interest to an inarticulate youth who was trying to fathom riddles in himself and cope with forebodings of the world about him. High daring, deep melancholy, ambition, anger, and wild defiance speak to the soul of youth—especially when they are "judgmatically" salted and peppered throughout with a robust, skeptical, workingman's humor.

Youth longs to find life fair and good, yet inevitably it will encounter sordid impulses in itself and in others. Youth would like to believe that all is possible, but it cannot avoid observing how helplessly adults face their more serious problems. Youth has the wish to penetrate life's mysteries, but it finds itself being taught by learned men who are, as regards just these mysteries, know-nothings and believe-nothings. Above and beneath all, there is in most young persons a self-esteem and self-concern that are bruised by the indifference of the rest of humanity, all of whom have, of course, their own concerns. These conflicts between subjective idealism and objective reality are the very signature of young life trying, and failing, to find itself at home in the world. They explain why *Moby Dick* tallies the experience of many an adolescent; and who would want to say that in this meaning of the word he has entirely outgrown adolescence?

Throughout his lifetime of writing, Melville was preoccupied with the fact that what the ardent self brings forward out of itself as ideals is apparently not to be reconciled with the harsh realities encountered in the external world. This discrepancy forms the substance of most of the books before and after *Moby Dick*, but in this particular tragedy it comes to expression in a way that far transcends mere youthful, or private, distress.

I

Possibly the most important fact to remember about the story of *Moby Dick* is that it takes place on the water. The first chapter, "Loomings," opens with an attempt to remind us of the obscure but deeply rooted feelings that bodies of water awaken at times in the human heart and mind. Water is undeniably a magnet for the soul of any man who feels himself to be something more than of the earth. Somehow water contains mysteries towards which we land-bound human beings feel ourselves drawn. In it we sense possibilities of enlargement, even enlightenment. Water opens perspectives of an inward kind. It helps one to a broader, deeper capacity of realization. “As everyone knows,” says Melville, “water and meditation are wedded forever.” (3)

Meditative, imaginative forms of knowing bear the same relation to water as the logic of everyday bears to solid ground. Water is the symbol of the living, creative power of thought that sometimes fills us like a tide, lifting us out of everyday pre-occupations, and opens our vision to more spiritual forces, presences, and events. To make an extended journey on the face of the greatest of all waters is therefore to venture, at all risk, into the unknown wonders of the soul, of nature, and of destiny.

Historically, the self-conscious, reasoning mind has arisen, as an island may rise from the sea, out of the impersonality of dreaming instinct and impulse. In this sense, the primitive water-consciousness is a thing we have done well to leave behind and below us. On the other hand, there is reason to believe that a higher kind of water-consciousness will be required by the future. The mentality with which our present world is attempting unsuccessfully to manage its affairs has grown stiff and hard. It is drying out. Only the moisture of new life will restore to it the powers of insight and creativeness it needs. One has the impression, from this perspective, that Melville's state of mind while writing *Moby Dick* was partly of the past, partly of the future. It was in part a subnormal dreaming consciousness, yet also a supernormal kind of prophesying.

Melville speaks of the whale as “this Leviathan” who “comes floundering down upon us from the headwaters of the Eternities.” Of what kind were those waters? In Genesis, when we read of darkness upon the deep, and the spirit of God moving upon the face of the waters, thought-habit probably brings to mind an image of darkest night surrounding the earth planet and its oceans. But there was no earth planet then, and there were no oceans: neither substance nor form of any kind. Nor, for that matter, was there a sun to be hidden, causing darkness. Earth and ocean, sun and stars, according to the first book of Moses, were all fashioned much later. In the primal beginning, there were only the mysterious ‘waters’— and the firmament called heaven that “divided the waters from the waters.” And the waters under heaven were gathered to become an earth planet and the oceans of such a planet. But what of the other waters, those which remained 'above' the firmament of heaven? Moses must have visualized these as being of a spiritual nature: some kind of purely ideal yet living source out of which all the heavenly bodies could be formed and by which they could continue to be nourished.

Primordial, living, ensouled world-thought must be pictured when we think of the waters through which swims the power of the white whale Melville has in view. And as there are waters and waters, so must there be whales and whales. "Who can show a pedigree like Leviathan? . . . I am horror-struck at this antemosaic, unsourced existence of the unspeakable terrors of the whale, which, having been before all time, must needs exist after all humane ages are over." (454) But more of Leviathan later.

Not only the rhythms and imagery of Melville's writing but also his concepts ask of the reader that he loosen the hold of solid matter upon his mind and entrust himself to a more buoyant, more far-ranging and deeper-diving consciousness. A simple consideration will suggest what is required if we are to feel at home in Melville's water-world.

We know that the modern man, lifted out high and dry, as it were, from the flowing life of nature, is a self-conscious, self-directing, indeed self-centered person. Each of us tends to be a law unto himself. In this sense, each person may be compared to a stone whose force of coherence holds it together as a thing in itself, apart from and excluding other things. We know that our attention moves outward into the world from that centerpoint in ourselves that we call the self or ego. Our consciousness is sharp and clear: its goal, as we say, is to be crystalline. Consciousness is seated in the head; and even as the head is the compact, still part of the body, so the consciousness with which we conduct usual affairs is not content until it has brought the ceaseless flux of events to a similar standstill: that is, has defined every separate object and pinned it by its law. We modern men impose upon the flow of life our static perceptions.

But abstract concepts are not the only way in which we show our preference for fixity. We are accustomed also to seek for confirmation of reality through that most material of the senses, the sense of touch. Our 'understanding' wants always to plant its feet on the bedrock of physically tangible evidence. Because I sense, for example, that my writing paper rests on the blotter, the blotter on the desk, the desk on the floor, the floor on the foundations of my house, the foundations on subsoil, and the subsoil at last on granite, I feel that I understand the facts of my situation, and that all are well based.

But when we begin to inquire in this way about any kind of physical reality, there always remains a further step to be taken. Once we have grounded a preliminary fact in more basic facts, have dug down to the root-fact on which all others appear to rest—in the case of the paper on my desk, down to the undoubted granite—can we refrain from asking further: "On what does the root-fact—presently, the solid earth-mass itself—rest?" And now we come face to face with a non-fact, for the inconceivably ponderous earth is not resting on anything at all! This enormous rock appears to be floating like a feather in the world ether.

Suddenly, we are disoriented. The ever-solider basis from which we had been accustomed to draw our sense of assurance has evaporated. To discover what continues to hold things in place, we can no longer think in the manner of stones that always settle towards the final bottom. Cosmically, there is no such bottom. There is only empty 'context.' Not substance but relationships are what count now. These relationships no longer point inwards towards the earth-center, but outwards to all parts of the world-periphery. The unspeakably heavy earth-ball floats serenely in a sea of mere relationships. "O, vast Rondure, swimming in space!" exclaimed Whitman. "How like a whale!" might have been Melville's rejoinder.

When we leave earthbound experience and venture imaginatively into cosmic space, we must accustom ourselves to a new way of looking at things. This new way derives its assurance from the feeling of buoyancy, even as the old way rested upon solidity and weight. With this buoyant new consciousness we can appreciate what it means for the earth to swim in the world ether—and we can begin to reconsider events on the earth itself that we had hitherto studied only in the old way.

Regardless of what the eminently successful launchers of physical space-flight will say to our cavalier treatment of how the earth swims only by relationship to her sister planets in the cosmos, this way of speaking may serve to conjure up a certain feeling that is, in fact, related to the psychological experience of water as Melville intends for us to experience it. Thoreau had this feeling when he said that in floating on Walden Pond he became a citizen of the cosmos. He could believe himself set free from gravity and placed in orbit as a small world in space—the neighboring worlds being felt no longer as remote and easy to forget but as intimately near and living.

By becoming individuals, by learning to walk each his own way, modern human beings have torn themselves partly out of the universal continuum, and have thereby lost their buoyancy. "Men of little faith," said Thoreau, "stand only by their feet." Yet Thoreau knew that it is possible to be a modern man, retain individuality, and yet learn to regain buoyant rapport with the All. His experience at Walden Pond is a good preparation for Melville's great adventure. "When most at one with nature," he said, "I feel supported and propped on all sides." (*Journal*, 1840)

Nature grows, evolves, transforms itself, begets new life, within the all-sustaining buoyancy of the universal context. This it can do only because it is liquid: fluency is life; fixity, death. And though the death-process (witness the rigid skull, which crystallizes whatever it captures for cognition) may bring man to his ordinary self-consciousness, it obviously cannot grasp the essence of life. For life is to be apprehended only by a consciousness that has reestablished its fluent cosmic rapport. Said Emerson:

> It is a secret which every intellectual man quickly learns, that beyond the energy of his possessed and conscious intellect he is capable of a new energy (as of an intellect doubled on itself), by abandonment to the nature of things; that beside his privacy of power as an individual man, there is a great public power on which he can draw, by unlocking, at all risks, his human doors, and suffering the ethereal tides to roll and circulate through him. . . . ("The Poet" p. 332)

The ethereal tides are those of living thought. Through this kind of thought, said Emerson, man is caught up into the creative spiritual life of the cosmos. He comes, said Melville, to "the headwaters of the Eternities."

II

If we may assume, then, that this whaling story means to launch us on what, for poetic imagination, become the seas of inward experience, what is the goal of the voyage upon which we are to embark? On the third page, Melville offers the clue. In venturing upon the great ocean, he says, when the last bit of land has dropped wholly out of sight, a man is likely to feel overtaken by a "mystical vibration": somehow he stands before, or in the very midst of, the mystery of existence; existence in general, but also his own in particular. Melville is reminded of the Greek myth of the fair youth Narcissus,

> who because he could not grasp the tormenting, mild image he saw in the fountain, plunged into it and was drowned. But that same image, we ourselves see in all rivers and oceans. It is the image of the un-graspable phantom of life; and this is the key to it all. (3)

This is the key! In what sense is the story of self-enamored Narcissus the story of Ahab also, in his fatal fascination with Moby Dick?

To answer this question, we must understand one peculiarity of imaginative experience. The imagination is fluid and makes fluid. It turns all things to self-transforming water. But water is a mirror, and like a mirror it reverses whatever it reflects. In genuine imagination as in many dreams, this strange reversal takes place. We discern that what seems to us as dreamers to be approaching from outside is actually welling up within ourselves. And even as the imagination holds up a mirror to life, there is a sense in which life itself is a great imagination, and thus a mirror for every human soul that passes through it. Does not the man who walks forward with habitual gratitude encounter an uncommon number of people and events towards which he can be grateful? Does not the suspicious or stingy man pass through an uncommon number of events that seem to want to rob or gyp him? Does not the stubborn bruiser strike his head against one solid wall after another that rises before him as before no one else?

We must suppose that what Narcissus saw in the mirror pool of his imagination was the mystery of his own being, and that this revelation overwhelmed him through the self-love it awakened. He could not hold himself back from the fatal wish to plunge into the wellsprings of his own nature. We may well believe that the resulting self-immersion left him as one dead to the rest of the world. Certainly, Melville was like Narcissus, in being profoundly concerned with himself. He was irresistibly drawn to dive for ever deeper levels in his own soul. As Hawthorne testified in dismay, on the basis of his personal friendship with Melville, he was what we may call a metaphysical plunger.

Melville's early years of seafaring gave him ample chance to indulge the over-mastering propensity to brood. Through words he puts into the mouth of Ishmael, the narrator of the story *Moby Dick*, we get an idea of what no doubt had often transpired when he took his turn in standing watch aloft at the masthead. Though his assigned task was to look outward for physical whales in the physical ocean, he appears more often to have used these occasions to look inward for imaginations swimming through the bottomless waters of pure thought. "With the problem of the universe revolving in me," Ishmael says, "how could I—being left completely to myself at such a thought-engendering altitude—how could I but lightly hold my obligations . . .?" (156)

Conjuring nautical music as ever, Melville conveys this experience of the young man, both romantic and melancholy, who is sent aloft to look sharp:

> . . . lulled into such an opium-like listlessness of vacant, unconscious reverie is this absent-minded youth by the blending cadence of waves with thoughts, that at last he loses his identity; takes the mystic ocean at his feet for the visible image of that deep, blue, bottomless soul, pervading mankind and nature; and every dimly-discovered, uprising fin of some undiscernible form, seems to him the embodiment of those elusive thoughts that only people the soul by continually flitting through it . . . (157)

There is no life in the mainmast sentinel now, "except that rocking life imparted by a gently rolling ship; by her, borrowed from the sea; by the sea, from the inscrutable tides of God." In this enchanted mood, Melville says, the conscious spirit "ebbs away to whence it came; becomes diffused through time and space; like Cranmer's sprinkled Pantheistic ashes, forming at last a part of every shore the round globe over . . ." (157)

We should not pass by this description too quickly, because it shows us something about Melville's constitution that accounted for the quality of his life-experience, which in turn provided the substance for his writing. The ability to dwell as Melville-Ishmael did in living thought is not a brain-based but a body-free experience: that is, a purely self-sustaining spiritual activity. Emerson speaks of the need an abstract thinker has for "periods of isolation and rapt concentration": "almost a going out of the body in order to think." ("Wealth," 711) At such moments "the intellect goes out of the individual, floats over its own personality, and regards it as a fact, and not as *I* or *mine*." ("Intellect," 292-3) This higher level of thinking "rends the thin rinds of the visible and finite, and comes out into eternity, and inspires and expires its air." ("The Over-Soul," 266) The soul of man then follows its "centrifugal tendency," finds "passage out into free space," and is enabled to "escape the custody of that body in which he is pent up, and that jailyard of individual relations in which he is enclosed." ("The Poet," 332-3)

Whitman testified to the same experience: "I loosen myself," he said, and "pass freely." (*Leaves of Grass*, 160) "I fly the flight of the fluid and swallowing soul . . . I help myself to material and immaterial . . ." (105) "My ties and ballasts leave me—I travel—I sail—my elbows rest in the sea-gaps; I skirt the sierras—my palms cover continents . . ." (100)

As we have noted, Melville was much inclined towards this *expansion* of consciousness, and the monotonous life at sea further developed the tendency. Later in *Moby Dick* he continues his characterization of how the susceptible consciousness of the narrator of the story, young Ishmael as he stood watch on high, was conjured out of itself by the unlimited sea at his feet.

> No resolution could withstand it; in that dreamy mood losing all consciousness, at last my soul went out of my body; though my body still continued to sway as a pendulum will, long after the power which first moved it is withdrawn. (283)

But Ishmael had the security of his perch on the mast to hold him intact. He was aloft in the air yet still aboard ship; else his experience might have been the one Melville ascribed to poor, lost Pip, the castaway black cabin boy who during a chase jumped from his whale boat and was soon left a mile behind, completely alone on the shoreless ocean. Pip's soul was swallowed up by the boundless waters.

Melville had a basis in himself for knowing what Pip's experience was like: "The intense concentration of self in the middle of such a heartless immensity, my God! Who can tell it?" (312) The castaway, alone on the surface of the deep, found that his "ringed horizon began to expand around him miserably." His self was sucked out of itself. Though his finite body survived, "the infinite of his soul" was drowned; that is, it could not recover itself from its over-expansion. It could not resume its self-possession or regain a proper footing on earth, after having been transported into the cosmic world of living thought. The passage is worth quoting, because it is so typically Melvillean both in power of language and in its incalculable overtones. Pip's soul, says Melville, was

> carried down alive to wondrous depths, where strange shapes of the unwarped primal world glided to and fro before his passive eyes; and the miser-merman, Wisdom, revealed his hoarded heaps; and among the joyous, heartless, ever-juvenile eternities, Pip saw the multitudinous, God-omnipresent, coral insects, that out of the firmament of waters heaved the colossal orbs. He saw God's foot upon the treadle of the loom, and spoke it; and therefore his shipmates called him mad. So man's insanity is heaven's sense; and wandering from all mortal reason, man comes at last to that celestial thought, which to reason, is absurd and frantic; and weal or woe, feels then uncompromised, indifferent as his God. (413)

III

We now have a basis, not a solid but a watery basis, on which to suggest some of the meanings of *Moby Dick* as a projection of tendencies in the soul of its author—and perhaps also as a prophecy concerning tendencies in his native land. Having seen how Melville could portray a Pip's relationship to the world, we turn our attention to Ahab—Ahab who said that Pip bore the same relationship to him "as the circumference to its center." (524)

If Pip represents the extreme of the centrifugal tendency Melville felt in his own soul, Ahab represents the extreme development of its opposite, the centripetal pull. Because both were extreme, both came to madness: "One daft with strength (Ahab), the other daft with weakness (Pip)," as the old Manxman said. Their madnesses were similar and symmetrical, in that they had to do with a disordered relation of the ego to its experience of spiritual reality; yet they were polarically opposed, in that in Pip's case the self was too emptied of itself, and in Ahab's case it was too filled with itself.

All of Melville's writing is based upon polarities of this kind. As in the forms of Pip and Ahab he described the modern ego in opposite ways, so the particular experience confronted by the ego, namely Moby Dick, the great white whale, cannot be fathomed by a single interpretation; it too must be studied in dual form. Moby Dick was a qualitative experience of the soul of Ahab, seen in the mirror of imaginative reality. But I should like to suggest that Ahab's soul, at different stages of its development, as he changed in his own nature from youth to age and from one kind of ego-experience to its opposite, saw two radically different whales.

The legendary white whale is the projection of two contrasting kinds of experience in the soul of the mad captain of the whaling ship *Pequod.* What precisely were those experiences? Can they be translated from the language of water to the language of land—that is, from images to concepts?

Narcissus looked into the pool, saw himself, and was fatally attracted. Ahab looked into his much larger pool, and was equally obsessed by what he saw. He saw the essential in himself as a great white whale; but since, as we shall try to make clear, the essential in him was *the conflict between polaric tendencies,* the whale that he pursued, the whale that came against him, also partook alternately of two natures, the one developing alongside or out of the other. This unsuspected duality has introduced confusion into all simplistic attempts to interpret what is going on between Ahab and Moby Dick. We may begin to appreciate what is involved here if we visualize a certain sequence of experiences known to many a young man of modern times. Let us observe an 'Ishmael' before he turns into an 'Ahab.'

Our hypothetical young man starts life as an idealist. He is ardent, ambitious, proud. He feels in himself giant possibilities. If he has the stature of a Melville-Ishmael, the young man may, indeed, be quite overwhelmed with dreams of beauty and grandeur, of moral elevation and spiritual power. Yet this young romanticist is not at home either in himself or in the world, for he is given also to doubt and despair. We see him brooding morbidly, self-absorbed, ready to be hurt. In this first phase he is innocent, impulsive, moved by passionately good intentions; yet by turns dejected, melancholy, and overtaken by he knows not what shadow. Sometimes his eyes search the stars; at other times, they are downcast on the earth.

Now let us imagine the efforts of this highly endowed but somewhat morbid young man to make a place for himself in the conventional world. He may, of course, ignore the outside challenge and launch ever further into his private dreams of the ideal. On this tack, he will find himself increasingly alone with his own overheated fantasy, which may lead him to unbreathable heights, or to unsoundable depths. He will become a Pip, too disoriented to judge and too weak to do anything about the mysteries—or are they illusions?—in which his spirit dwells. If, however, the young man takes his way at least partly into the 'real' world, he will be shocked by what he encounters there: pettiness of spirit, violence and vileness. He will feel opposed by both persons and circumstances, appalled to find that what he thinks best in himself often seems to provoke the greatest antagonism in others. Eventually, he may come to feel that the world of men, the customs of society, the prevailing culture, above all the economic order, are worse than merely ignorant and unlovely: they may seem willfully deceitful and cruel. He cannot get on in such a world. He does not understand it but feels called upon to oppose it in outrage and as a matter of principle.

The young man so violently compressed may violently explode. If he is the kind of Ishmael that has the makings of an Ahab in him, his early pride will turn to burning resentment; his early ambition will become the desire for revenge; his once benevolent intelligence will be transformed into manic plotting.

If we walk another step with this young man who cannot help getting older even though he despises his elders, who must fight for a foothold in the very world he holds in contempt, and who cannot win except by the rules of a game that outrages him, we shall observe a remarkable change taking place in him. His initial egoism will persist, it will indeed be deepened; but it will take on quite another character: one that bears a close resemblance, whether he recognizes it or not, to the very traits in the established world that caused him such distress in the first place! It is now his own heart that has hardened. It is he himself who has become skeptical, shrewd and aggressive, in the vengeful belief that the world deserves nothing so much as a double dose of its own bitter medicine. He undertakes this cure, with a vengeance. He does not notice that he has been absorbed by the evil he thinks he is opposing! Ishmael has turned into Ahab.

Phase one tallies a good deal of what we know or can guess about the early character of Ahab, Ahab before he lost his leg and became so grim; and we may take the young Ahab to represent a basic, an original, aspect of Melville's own nature. In this aspect we see him starting out with a purely spiritual idealism and ambition. He is, as it were, born of light and he aspires to the light. This part of his nature continues as he grows older, but through the encounter with life's adversities it also changes. His light darkens into fire. He feels himself capable of storming heaven, a Prometheus who would steal fire from the gods. The original light and the eventual fire mingle confusingly.

It was the older Ahab who exclaimed, "Oh, thou clear spirit of clear fire, of thy fire thou madest me, and like a true child of fire, I breathe it back to thee"; (499) and in another context he soliloquizes, "Clear truth is a thing for salamander giants only." (377) Salamanders are fire beings, and Ahab considers himself such a one. He sees himself as Lucifer, the angel who though he started as the high bearer of light, fell to become the fiery dark spirit of pride:

> There's something ever egotistical in mountain-tops and towers, and all other grand and lofty things; look here—three peaks as proud as Lucifer. The firm tower, that is Ahab; the volcano, that is Ahab; the courageous, the undaunted, and victorious fowl, that, too, is Ahab; all are Ahab. . . . (428)

There is a proud eagle in some souls, he says,

> that can alike dive down into the blackest gorges, and soar out of them again and become invisible in the sunny spaces. And even if he forever flies within the gorge, that gorge is in the mountains; so that even in his lowest swoop the mountain eagle is still higher than other birds upon the plain, even though they soar. (423)

In the boundless ocean of spiritual pride and ambition, such an ego as Ahab would naturally pursue only the greatest of fish, the whale, and the greatest of whales, the legendary, ubiquitous, immortal

White Whale; for he is on the hunt for ultimate truth, the truth that is also highest power. "Unless you own the whale," Melville says, "you are but a provincial and sentimentalist in Truth." (337) "Speak," mutters Ahab to the severed Sphinx head hoisted alongside his ship. "Speak, thou vast and venerable head . . . speak, mighty head, and tell us the secret thing that is in thee. Of all divers thou hast dived the deepest." (310)

We find the Luciferic phase of Ahab's soul fitly pictured in this description of the White Whale's glory:

> A gentle joyousness—a mighty mildness of repose in swiftness, invested the gliding whale. Not the white bull Jupiter swimming away with ravished Europa clinging to his graceful horns; with smooth bewitching fleetness, rippling straight for the nuptial bower in Crete; not Jove, not that great majesty Supreme! did surpass the glorified White Whale as he so divinely swam. (537-8)

Such a whale mirrors the part of Ahab's aspiring idealism that sought to approach the primordial powers of beauty and truth which made the world—yet that partook also of ambitious pride and conceit.

But we know that what we are making free to call the Lucifer-phase of Ahab's young development was already past when the quest for Moby Dick, as told in this story, begins. The whale that now swam before the battered captain, in the seas that mirrored the radically changed condition of his soul, was a fundamentally different creature from the above-described. His essence had more to do with icy coldness than with seductive light and warmth; more to do with calculating power than with spiritual illumination. He was, indeed, the very epitome of "intelligent malignity."

> The White Whale swam before him as the monomaniac incarnation of all those malicious agencies which some deep men feel eating in them, till they are left living on with half a heart and half a lung. . . . All that most maddens and torments; all that stirs up the lees of things; all truth with malice in it; all that cracks the sinews and cakes the brain; all the subtle demonisms of life and thought; all evil, to crazy Ahab, were visibly personified, and made practically assailable in Moby Dick. He piled upon the whale's white hump the sum of all the general rage and hate felt by his whole race from Adam down; and then, as if his chest had been a mortar, he burst his hot heart's shell upon it. (183)

A "Khan of the plank, and a king of the sea and a great lord of Leviathans" such as Ahab cannot cease to play the Titan. But his battle with life has taken something away from him and introduced something new into him. His crippled willfulness now takes a vindictive, hateful turn, whose reflection is to be seen in the maimed aspect of Moby Dick: the "vast, involved wrinkles" of his forehead, the "terrors of his submerged trunk," and "the wrenched hideousness of his jaw." (539) These betray an "inscrutable malice," an "infernal aforethought of ferocity." (162, 182)

We must try to be more precise about this ambivalence, this shifting duality that makes Ahab and his mirror-image Moby Dick so hard to interpret. This same dualism, as we have said, pervades all of Melville's writing. *Moby Dick* was written between two other books: the earlier *Mardi* and the later *Pierre, or the Ambiguities.* In *Mardi,* a romantic quest by representatives of the philosophic, poetic, historical, and heroic aspects of the human soul—of Melville's own soul—is underway. Its goal: to find again and bring back the maiden of light, Yillah, who seems to have vanished. But the fellowship that is wandering in search of Yillah is itself being pursued by the queen of darkness, Hautia. In *Pierre,* the hero has promised his hand to Lucy, also a maiden of light; but the marriage does not take place, for Isabel, a raven-haired girl of tragic fate, intervenes. In both books, the conflict between light and darkness is the central theme.

In *Moby Dick,* the agents and their motives are equally ambiguous. Two basic tendencies in human nature, and perhaps in cosmic nature as well, are at war with each other for mastery of the captain's soul. Melville characterizes both in his chapter on "The Whiteness of the Whale."

IV

"But how can I hope to explain myself here," says Ishmael: "and yet, in some dim, random way, explain myself I must, else all these chapters might be naught." (187) The matter that needs explaining is how it could be that in the whiteness of the whale was to be felt simultaneously, or alternately, a spiritual beauty and a "nameless horror."

What is hard to understand is how the color white can arouse in the beholder two absolutely different sets of feelings. These feelings correspond to the two tendencies in human nature, or the two influences exerted upon man from beyond his own nature, that we are attempting to characterize. In the first instance, white is the color of divinity.

> . . . in the higher mysteries of the most august religions it has been made the symbol of the divine spotlessness and power; by the Persian fire worshippers, the white forked flame being held the holiest on the altar; and in the Greek mythologies, Great Jove himself being made incarnate in a snow white bull. . . . (187-8)

Yet for all its association with "celestial innocence and love," "there . . . lurks an elusive something in the innermost idea of this hue, which strikes more of panic to the soul than that redness which affrights in blood." (188) Here, says Melville, we are dealing with a matter "so mystical and well nigh ineffable" as almost to defy rational understanding: "subtlety appeals to subtlety, and without imagination no man can follow another into these halls." (191)

We must be imaginative and subtle, but we must also be exact at this point, lest Melville himself lead us away from understanding. The question is not as to which of the two aspects of whiteness, the glorious or the grisly, is the real one. The goal is not to convince ourselves that the innocent kind of whiteness is youthful illusion, behind which we shall, if we have enough grown-up courage to push on, discover the frightful nature that white 'really' is—even though this is the course taken by Ishmael's reflections. We are dealing not with illusion and truth but rather with two illusions, which is to say with two mutually opposed aspects of reality, neither of which represents complete and balanced truth.

White stands for light, and the first aspect of light that is under consideration here we can associate, as we have suggested, with Lucifer. It gives him his name. This whiteness speaks for the super-earthly; it draws us back towards earlier stages of spiritual development before mankind had taken on the weight of matter. It awakens the longing to escape from the earth: the desire to retreat into the white dress of untempted purity, or at least to don the priestly vestments of untouchable dignity and sacred esteem.

If this first kind of light, or whiteness, may be linked with any and all of the religions of ancient time, we must associate the second kind with the sterility of our modern laboratories and operating rooms, the abstractness of our post-mortem science. Melville, speaking through Ishmael, in his attempt to explain the coldness and emptiness of a certain kind of white light, builds towards just this conclusion.

> It cannot well be doubted, that the one visible quality of the dead which most appalls the gazer, is the marble pallor lingering there; as if indeed that pallor were as much like the badge of consternation in the other world, as of mortal trepidation here. (190-1)

The pallor of death, whether it appears on the face of a corpse, or in the "eternal, frosted desolateness" of solitary peaks in mountain fastnesses, or in the boundless, blizzard-swept graveyard of Antarctic ice-fields, is chilling. It is frightening.

> Is it that by its indefiniteness it shadows forth the heartless voids and immensities of the universe, and thus stabs us from behind with the thought of annihilation . . .? (194)

No doubt there are dread prospects to be seen here and there on earth, and inhuman solitudes to be endured by some; and death comes to all. But why should we ignore the warm beauties of nature as they surround us on every side, in order to quake and shiver about desolate wastes of whiteness rarely seen? And why should we regard death as final annihilation? How do we know the immensities of the universe are heartless?

"Not yet," says Ishmael, "have we solved the incantation of this whiteness." (194)

> Though in many of its aspects this visible world seems formed in love, the invisible spheres were formed in fright. (194)

That is, they were formed in chill abstraction, apart from wisdom, or love, or even purpose. The beauty and warmth that naive men think they are encountering in nature and in destiny are but appearances. They may seem to be everywhere present, but this proves only that illusions wrap us on all sides. The reality that lies behind them is not beautiful, because it is not warm, not colored, not odorous, not sounding. At least, we shall be convinced that this is the case if we accept what many scientists have had to tell us about the nature of all our sensory perceptions.

Newton did as much as any man to tear away the veil mankind had seen as "the starry heavens," and to expose the universe as pure mechanism. And by the time *Moby Dick* was published, Darwin had begun the explanation of how plants, animals, and men develop in such a universe: by a fight to the death of all against all, with advantage falling to this one or that according to the heartless, unthinking chances of purely random mutations. Long ago, Galileo had laid down a fundamental distinction between what he called the primary, or real, and the secondary or only apparent attributes of things. Secondary are heat, light, color, sound, taste, odor. All these are subjective: that is, they exist only in the supposition of the beholder who prefers to make believe that they are there. Primary and real are such featureless, unimaginable, alien abstractions as pure mass, shape, and velocity. Though such concepts are everywhere accepted by the philosophers of science, and though they account for the faithless outlook of the modern world, the average layman of today still ignores them. Out of a healthy instinct to protect himself—through ignorance if necessary—against things frightful, the layman holds such ideas away from his feeling-life. But for a poet, a bold soul and partly a morbid one such as Melville, they strike home in the heart.

If Newton's idea of color be true, thought Melville, and Galileo's distinction between the *reality* of unseen, mechanical abstractions and the *unreality* of our most clearly received, most comforting and inspiring human perceptions, then "the palsied universe lies before us a leper." The soul who has courage to look facts in the face, to take off his "colored and coloring glasses" and see the workings of the world as they really are, is likely to go snow-blind, and stone-cold. The paragraph with which Melville concludes his chapter on the whiteness of the whale is worth quoting almost in its entirety:

> Or is it, that as in essence whiteness is not so much a color as the visible absence of color; and at the same time the concrete of all colors; is it for these reasons that there is such a dumb blankness, full of meaning, in a wide landscape of snows—a colorless, all-color of atheism from which we shrink? And when we consider that other theory of the natural philosophers, that all other earthly hues—every stately or lovely emblazoning—. . . all these are but subtile deceits, not actually inherent in substances, but only laid on from without; so that all deified

> Nature absolutely paints like the harlot, whose allurements cover nothing but the charnel house within; and when we proceed further, and consider that the mystical cosmetic which produces every one of her hues, the great principle of light, for ever remains white or colorless in itself, and if operating without medium upon matter, would touch all objects, even tulips and roses, with its own blank tinge—pondering all this, the palsied universe lies before us a leper; and like willful travellers in Lapland, who refuse to wear colored and coloring glasses upon their eyes, so the wretched infidel gazes himself blind at the monumental white shroud that wraps all the prospect around him. And of all these things the Albino whale was the symbol. Wonder ye then at the fiery hunt? (194-5)

When Coleridge had studied Newton's *Optics* thoroughly, he exclaimed, "Everything fits so perfectly; the reasoning is faultless! It *must* be wrong." Goethe recognized in Newton's optics simply an example of one way of interpreting the phenomena of nature. He considered that way, though in certain respects useful, to be fatally reductionist and therefore fundamentally unreal. He believed that if scientific inquiry were to continue to explain qualitative phenomena in this style, it would lay waste the entire world, not only for inner human experience but also ultimately in its practical consequences. "May God us keep from single vision and Newton's sleep!" wrote Blake in a letter to Thomas Butts.

Coleridge, Goethe, and Blake, out of an instinct for reality, rejected the mechanistic world-outlook that held a morbid fascination for Melville. They saw it as illusion, because it was the product of a one-sided application of human intelligence. This maimed, this unnatural and inhuman outlook, Melville personified in the older Ahab. The dire captain comes before us not perhaps as one-eyed in his vision, but certainly as one-legged in his understanding.

Ahab, in what we have called his second phase, though the story opens with him already in this condition, represents highest intellectual development pushed on by audacious, relentless will.

> What is it, what nameless, inscrutable, unearthly thing is it; what cozening, hidden lord and master, and cruel, remorseless emperor commands me; that against all natural lovings and longings, I so keep pushing, and crowding, and jamming myself on all the time; recklessly making me ready to do what

> in my own proper, natural heart, I durst not so much as dare? Is Ahab, Ahab? (534-5)

Ahab attacks life and nature in this manner; and in the mirror that life holds up to him he sees a certain kind of monster on the counter-attack. This monster is the image of his own attitude; but his own attitude is borrowed in turn from concepts that scientific materialists of the nineteenth century had put forward as to the nature of the universe man lives in: brute power and mechanism that have somehow managed to spawn men and women of tenderest feelings and noblest aspirations; that beguile mankind, indeed, with illusions of beauty, truth, and goodness, only to wipe them out, illusions and all—with complete indifference, if such a thing be imaginable; or if not, with "inscrutable malice." Is it any wonder that the smoldering pride in Ahab should be enraged?

> All visible objects, man, are but as pasteboard masks. But in each event—in the living act, the undoubted deed—there, some unknown but still reasoning thing puts forth the mouldings of its features from behind the unreasoning mask. If man will strike, strike through the mask! How can the prisoner reach outside except by thrusting through the wall. To me the white whale is that wall, shoved near to me. . . . I see in him outrageous strength, with an inscrutable malice sinewing it. That inscrutable thing is chiefly what I hate; and be the white whale agent, or be the white whale principal, I will wreak that hate upon him. (162)

Ahab in his deep longings, his spiritual ambition, his will to glory, is antique: a Prometheus, a Lucifer. But in his *thwarted* longing and *wounded* pride he accepts a modern inspiration. He enters upon the ruthless will to power, power as served by the cold-blooded intellect. He is assimilated by a principle that stands wholly opposite to Lucifer. As Lucifer is a spirit of warmth and light, though a false one, this other being is a spirit of chill and frosty darkness. Ahab does not, of course, recognize this spirit as arising out of his own character, but he sees it attacking him from outside through Moby Dick. This is the spirit of "all truth with malice in it; all that cracks the sinews and cakes the brain":

> That intangible malignity which has been from the beginning; to whose dominion even the modern Christians ascribe one-half of the worlds; which the ancient Ophites of the east reverenced in their statue devil;—Ahab did not fall down and

> worship it like them; but deliriously transferring its idea to the abhorred white whale, he pitted himself, all mutilated, against it. (183)

V

To gain a clearer idea of who it is that pulls mankind in the opposite direction from Lucifer, we must take account of a too-little-noticed feature of *Moby Dick*: namely, the fact that it is through and through a story in the mood of ancient Persia. In *Mardi,* Melville had said: "My memory is a life beyond birth;" and "Zoroaster whispered me before I was born." In *Moby Dick,* we start out with the observer-narrator Ishmael, a Persian name. Captain Ahab's personal whaleboat crew and harpooneer are all Parsee, that is, Persian fire-worshippers. This crew lurks below decks in the after-hold—which for our purpose means deep in the subconscious—where Ahab is seen mysteriously visiting them in the dark of night. The Parsee leader, Fedallah, is from beginning to end the inspiring, controlling spirit behind Ahab, his prophetic voice of doom. "Though it come to the last," Fedallah says, "I shall still go before thee thy pilot." (491)

> At times, for longest hours, without a single hail, they stood far parted in the starlight; Ahab in his scuttle, the Parsee by the mainmast; but still fixedly gazing upon each other; as if in the Parsee Ahab saw his forethrown shadow, in Ahab the Parsee his abandoned substance. (527).

Melville goes to considerable lengths in various ways to make of Fedallah an almost disembodied being, a shadow who never sleeps and who is almost infinitely old—whose origin lies far back in time. He was felt by the ship's crew to be the devil himself.

As the chase is driving towards its climax off Japan, the *Pequod* runs into a typhoon.

> When darkness came on, sky and sea roared and split with thunder, and blazed with lightning. . . . All the yard-arms were tipped with pallid fire; and touched at each tri-pointed lightning-rod-end with three tapering white flames, each of the three tall masts was silently burning in that sulphurous air like three gigantic wax tapers before an altar. (495-7)

Ahab seizes the mainmast lightning-rod links in his left hand, places his foot on the prostrate Parsee, raises his eyes and right hand upward to the white flames, and utters these words:

> Oh! thou clear spirit of clear fire, whom on these seas I as Persian once did worship, till in the sacramental act so burned by thee, that to this hour I bear the scar; I now know thee, thou clear spirit, and I know now that thy right worship is defiance. To neither love nor reverence wilt thou be kind; and e'en for hate thou canst but kill; and all are killed. (499)

In some way the mysterious but compelling story of *Moby Dick* is rooted in the religious concepts and world-conception of ancient Persia. Before offering what I think Melville himself believed about this fact, I should like to say a word about the religion of Persia, founded many thousand years before the time of Christ by Zarathustra, or Zoroaster. This inspirer of Persian culture, and through it, later, of the Hebrew and Greek cultures, taught that world-reality is divided into two aspects, the light and the dark. The prince of darkness and falsehood he called Angra Mainyu, or Ahriman. The spirit of light and truth, the great aura of the sun, he called Ahura Mazdao, or Ormazd. The spirit of the depths of darkness was conceived as working ever to entangle men in matter. The spirit of heavenly heights strove to hold them free of matter. Ahura Mazdao was revered as the primordial spirit of creative goodness, but perhaps the conception of his nature also included unrecognized elements of the Luciferic. At any rate, the particular spirit of death and evil with which Ahab in his later phase identified Moby Dick was clearly identified. Let us call him, as the Persians did, Ahriman.

In terms of present-day experience, we could say that Lucifer holds man aloof from the common lot and common sense of humanity on earth; makes of him a visionary, earth-estranged, overheated spiritualist. Ahriman, however, sucks man too deeply into the earth experience; makes of him a shrewd, heartless and power-seeking materialist. What Melville sought was the Golden Mean, the way that lies between them. But to balance the forces of light and darkness, as he strove unsuccessfully to do, what is necessary is a triadic rather than a dualistic world view. The third reality, the reconciling, harmonizing, truly human factor, is to be looked for in or through the heart. This inspiration of the center, which stands in freedom between the polar opposites that ever draw a man off balance with himself, Melville thought to find, as he acknowledged at the conclusion of his earlier book, *Mardi,* in the one who was both Son of Man and Son of God. In *Mardi,* Melville calls Christ "Alma," and the Mardian who in this book represented highest wisdom felt his search had led aright when he found Alma. But Taji, the Ishmael of *Mardi,* remained unreconciled. Something in him demanded that the quest be continued and intensified. The result we have in *Moby Dick.*

Returning to the last passage quoted: "Oh! thou clear spirit of clear fire whom on these seas I as Persian once did worship . . .," we can perhaps visualize something in Ahab's nature as disposed to approach the spirit of light 'Persian-style.' But how shall we understand *"I as Persian once"?* Shall Ahab have been in fact Persian 'once upon a time'—which, according to Melville's view, would have been in an earlier life—or do we have to do with Ahab in an earlier stage of his present life, behaving as a Parsee of old might have done? Perhaps there is something to be said for both interpretations; but what about: *"till in the sacramental act* so burned by thee, that to this day I bear the scar"?*

In *Moby Dick* mystery opens into mystery. I base my own interpretation of what the author intended concerning Ahab's deeper motivation upon Melville's numerous references, in this book and others to the idea of repeated earth lives (see for example Chapter 98, "Stowing Down and Clearing Up").† Unmistakable is the

---

* A close reader of *Moby Dick* might object that in Chapter 28 the question raised by Ahab's apostrophe to lightning is answered through the testimony of an old Gayhead Indian, who claimed that at an earlier time, when Ahab was about forty years of age, he had been struck and branded by lightning in a storm at sea. But this explanation of Ahab's 'vivid scar' (which is obviously more a spiritual symbol than a physical reality) is acknowledged to be a superstitious guess, rather than a statement of fact. Besides, if Melville really had in his own mind that Ahab's earlier encounter with cosmic light and fire had been simply a matter of being struck during a bad storm, even if vengefully struck, it seems most unlikely that he would have referred to the event as a "sacramental act." One cannot visualize that Ahab's mood was one of worship at such a time, or that he was performing sacred acts! Still less does the Gayhead Indian's assertion explain the phrase "I as Persian."

† In "The Idea of Man in America," *Proceedings* #28 of the Myrin Institute, Inc., pages 37-41, I have presented further evidence of Melville's interest and belief in the concept of repeated earth lives.

suggestion made in the early chapter where Melville first describes Ahab's relation to Moby Dick. In this chapter, after we have been shown how the whale represents the whole force of darkness and evil operating both in cosmic nature and in the destiny of mankind; and have been persuaded that Ahab was obsessed by his resentment of the whale both for its personal injury to him and for its portents of hurt to all men; how shall we account for the first sentence in the very next paragraph?

> This is much; yet Ahab's larger, darker, deeper part remains unhinted. (184)

How, indeed, account for the entire paragraph, which goes on to supply the mysterious hint that is to outweigh everything that has yet been said?

We are asked to visualize the situation. All that has been said of Ahab's relationship to the whale is not more, says Melville, than the description of a grand and wonderful "Hotel de Cluny" such as was the architectural and artistic wonder of the European Middle Ages. Melville has permitted us to enter this great building and penetrate to its heart, but he now invites us to start the descent from this very heart into the deeper foundations upon which the whole edifice rests. Make this descent-through-time, "ye nobler, sadder souls," and you will approach the real secret of what you want to know! Observe that you are now carried back to an earlier age. The medieval Hotel de Cluny rests upon Roman foundations, built to supply heat for the Roman baths that were once here. In these halls, "far beneath the fantastic towers of man's upper earth,"

> his root of grandeur, his whole awful essence sits in bearded state; an antique buried beneath antiquities, and throned on torsoes! so with a broken throne, the great gods mock that captive king; so like a Caryatid, he patient sits, upholding on his frozen brow the piled entablatures of ages. (184-5)

Melville suggests that what is true of Ahab is equally true of any soul that feels within itself a deep ego-problem, a baffling life-riddle. Every such soul must go back in time, to find the real secret of his destiny:

> Wind ye down there, ye prouder, sadder souls! question that proud, sad king! A family likeness! aye, he did beget ye, ye young exiled royalties; and from your grim sire only will the old State secret come. (185)

According to the teaching of reincarnation, which Melville felt to be confirmed by his own inward experience, the positive fruits of one life on earth are carried over, in some form, into the next. One can work with them and build upon them—a supposition that could go far to explain how a twenty-eight to thirty-year old youth of very little education, quite out of the blue, could write such books as *Mardi* and *Moby Dick*; but incomplete or negative experiences are also carried over, and these too must be further worked upon, for better or for worse. This is the idea Melville brings forward as the key of keys to Ahab's quest—Ahab standing no doubt for a single aspect of Melville himself.

One has the impression that in the present life, when he appears on the horizon of our present story, Ahab is to a large extent a man of his time. That is, he is an aggressive, intellectual, godless exploiter of nature: he follows Ahriman. But at heart he is still bemused by Lucifer. One can speculate, however, that it was in a past life of critical importance that his destiny received its characteristic stamp. Permitting ourselves to think freely for the moment in the idiom of ancient Persia, we may imagine him as an overly zealous disciple, or even priest, of some mystery school: fanatical in his devotions, let us say, but motivated too much by ambition. Walking the path he presumed to be that of spiritual development, at a certain stage he stumbled. Because he was already far along, his fall was more than an ordinary failure. Having confused imperious personal ardor with the true devotion that is patient and never personal, and having been rejected of the spirit, his soul was deeply confounded. And if his fault was even the cause of his death—a possibility not to be discounted, when we consider the absolute rigor of the ancient practices—so that he was struck down in his embittered condition while still far from any thought of making amends, we must suppose that in a following life his struggle to regain self-assurance would take him through the most uncertain and tempestuous conditions. We can believe that he would start out with the feeling that he had been maimed, but for unknown reasons. He would bear a grudge against life that could not be explained on contemporary grounds. He would feel that joy in living, and success, had been taken from him by a hand he could not identify, according to a logic he could not grasp. He would have lost his footing, been left with only one leg to stand on.

Such a man would be hard put to it to appreciate the workings of divine Providence! He would be tempted, rather, to believe that the course of events was even more malevolent than meaningless. He would wander through life as an outsider, rejected and rejecting. And with his fiery temperament, he would rage against the unfair treatment fate had accorded him.

If our scenario for Ahab be accepted as it is meant, as pure fiction yet helpful in picturing the causative *principle* behind Ahab's profound alienation, we shall not find it strange that his next life should to some extent have to repeat the mistakes of the earlier one.* In the former time, he failed because his devotion to the spirit had in it too much of personal ambition. In the present life, he fails because his vaunted independence is built too much upon antagonism and opposition. He is *against* something outside himself, but *for* nothing of his own. His original ambition, his first attempt as it were to curry favor with the spirit, had showed a lack of self-dependence. When, out of disappointment, ambition now turns to blame and hate, the mistake might seem to be of a different kind, yet it is still the same old failure in self-dependence. Though he proclaims proud defiance of gods and men, he is in no sense his own man. He cannot be quiet, cannot make sound judgments, cannot enjoy, cannot create. He is completely beside himself. The secret of freedom on which love is based, and the secret of love on which true freedom is based, he has yet to learn.

> . . . all loveliness is anguish to me, since I can ne'er enjoy. Gifted with the high perception, I lack the low enjoying power; damned, most subtly and most malignantly! damned in the midst of Paradise! (166)

The implications of the above hypothesis for Melville himself are that he may well have felt that the past he suggests for Ahab was actually his own. Perhaps he has these very mistakes to do penance for, and this very lesson to learn. As a writer, he could, by projecting and objectifying the problem of spiritual pride and ambition in the

---

* Let me emphasize, if emphasis be needed, that my suppositions have not been intended as a way of trying to arrive at truth by guesswork. They are meant only to dramatize and bring alive a riddle that we cannot solve, but neither can we ignore. Not the *fact* but the *style* of the matter is of concern here.

shape of Captain Ahab, advance his understanding of his own nature and consider how to overcome it.

VI

In the remarkable chapter entitled "The Lee Shore," Melville epitomizes much of what we have attributed to him, and to Ahab as an aspect of himself, in the matter of temperament, motivation, and problematic destiny. He pictures a man who cannot rest on the land of conventional truth, including conventional religious beliefs, but must ever and ever again drive outwards from all safe harbors into the unknown perils of the sea. On the one hand, this man is a spiritual hero, because he spurns every comfort of the "treacherous, slavish shore"; in his quest for ultimate truths he prefers to brave "the lashed sea's landlessness," even though this bring him to a tempestuous death. For,

> as in landlessness alone resides highest truth, shoreless, indefinite as God—so better is it to perish in that howling infinite, than be ingloriously dashed upon the lee, even if that were safety! For worm-like, then, oh! who would craven crawl to land! (105-6)

On the other hand, the tormented man pictured so briefly in this "six-inch" chapter fools himself when he believes that it is truth he is seeking. *Does* truth reside in "landlessness alone," where the knower is quite swallowed by what he would prematurely know; or is it to be found, rather, wherever a man who is at peace and at one with himself makes himself also at one with the object of his reverent wonder?

What we have called a heaven-stormer, a metaphysical plunger, is always led beyond himself. The courage for which he praises himself is actually a fatal conceit, and such a one never finds what he is looking for. He is led, or forced upon, one wild goose chase after another, by something in himself that remains unrecognized. Melville says that "all deep, earnest thinking is but the intrepid effort of the soul to keep the open independence of her sea," (105) but the compulsive plunger enjoys no such open independence. His presumptuous longings let him be sucked into the howling infinite, battered and beaten by it, until he and his are destroyed. His ambition is simply suicidal. And though Melville, in this particular case, ends by saying: "Take heart, take heart, . . . Up from the spray of thy ocean-perishing—straight up, leaps thy apotheosis!" (106), one cannot agree that willfulness is strength, and foolhardiness a higher form of courage. What leaps straight up from the fallen man is not himself as a god but Lucifer in triumph at the destructive success he has wrought.

Inordinate desire, even for the spiritual, disturbs the balance that is demanded by what Blake called "the human Form divine." Ambitious desire pulls a man away from what is harmonious and integral in himself, leaving him not more but less than human. Melville spoke more truly when in the later chapter on "Brit" he named the briny deep for what it is—for what the premature challenger will find it to be:

> No mercy, no power but its own controls it. Panting and snorting like a mad battle steed that has lost its rider, the masterless ocean overruns the globe. (275)

The ocean of morbid, driving introspection has nothing to do with the apotheosis of courage and independence. On the contrary, it unhorses every willful rider, and by its "universal cannibalism" swallows all that is best in him.

> Consider all this; and then turn to this green, gentle, and most docile earth; consider them both, the sea and the land; and do you not find a strange analogy to something in yourself? For as this appalling ocean surrounds the verdant land, so in the soul of man there lies one insular Tahiti, full of peace and joy, but encompassed by all the horrors of the half known life. God keep thee! Push not off from that isle, thou canst never return! (276)

It is because Ahab represents the part of Melville himself that did not want to heed this sound advice that the author could say of him:

> as touching all Ahab's deeper part, every revelation partook more of significant darkness than of explanatory light. (461)

And Ahab said of himself:

> So far gone am I in the dark side of earth, that its other side, the theoretic bright one, seems but uncertain twilight to me. (519-20)

Though Ahab in his youth, or in another life, may have sought transcendental light, when we encounter him as Captain of the *Pequod* he is sailing into the darkness of his own subconsciousness.

> Yet dost thou dark half, rock me with a prouder, if a darker faith. All thy unnamable imminglings float beneath me here... (490)
>
> And meet it is, that over these sea-pastures, wide-rolling watery prairies and Potter's Fields of all four continents, the waves should rise and fall, and ebb and flow unceasingly; for here, millions of mixed shades and shadows, drowned dreams, somnambulisms, reveries; all that we call lives and souls, lie dreaming, dreaming, still; tossing like slumberers in their beds; the ever-rolling waves but made so by their restlessness. (478)

It is worth noting at this point, in a book where all is parable, that the meditative waters in which Moby Dick is hunted are not fresh but salt. Of fresh water Thoreau had earlier written, "A lake . . . is the earth's liquid eye. . . . There it lies all the year, reflecting the sky—and from its surface there seems to go up a pillar of ether, which bridges over the space between earth and heaven. . . . Across the surface of every lake there sweeps a hushed music." (*Journal,* 1840) And in the chapter on "The Prairie," Melville compares the "clear, eternal, tideless mountain lakes" to the eyes of man, or at least to the eyes of geniuses who gaze upon the eternal: and he imagines "antlered thoughts descending there to drink." (345) Melville's observation coincided with Thoreau's: namely, that springs and lakes serve the earth as senses, through which it vividly perceives the cosmos. But the sea is salt; and if we think of the earth as a living cosmic being, as Melville said it was, and possessed of vital organs and functions, the salt seas must more resemble the abdomen than the head. In the great oceans, earth is withdrawn into its own metabolism, somnolent rather than awake; and the thoughts that course through its waters are dreams that grow progressively darker, the more deeply we penetrate into them.

> . . . to and fro in the deeps, far down in the bottomless blue, rushed mighty leviathans, sword-fish, and sharks; and these were the strong, troubled, murderous thinkings of the masculine sea. (531)

VII

The kind of hunt on which Ahab embarked *could* not succeed, for

> in pursuit of those far mysteries we dream of, or in tormented chase of that demon phantom that, some time or other, swims before all human hearts; while chasing such over this round globe, they either lead us on in barren mazes or midway leave us whelmed. (237)

In the end, a self-defeating strategy brought the *Pequod*, its captain, and all its crew except the observer, Ishmael, to ruin. We have already suggested some of the lessons Melville was teaching himself as an individual through the writing of this tragedy. It remains to ask why many commentators have felt that the parable of Ahab and the whale has dimensions that go far beyond the moral development of a single individual; why, indeed, it should be studied for prophetic clues to the destiny of the West, particularly America.

In order to test the hypothesis that *Moby Dick* is in a real sense the epic of our own America, which sets the pace for Western culture, let us begin by assuming it. The *Pequod* then becomes the American ship of state. Aboard is a polyglot mixture of nationalities, starting from a 'mongrel' base of renegades and castaways symbolized by the anonymous crew, and rising through several grades of those who begin to carry responsibility, as personified in the petty officers, Flask, Stubb and Starbuck; and commanded at last by one whose overweening, obsessive, ever-intensifying purpose either enlisted or swept aside all other wills. The good ship America carries a proletariat, a petit bourgeoisie, and an upper-middle, cultured, ruling class. It includes so-called advanced peoples, who do not distinguish themselves (the mates), and peoples called primitive because they remain closer to the origins of life (the harpooneers), who do comport themselves with distinction.

Fittingly, Melville characterizes the dramatic personnel in this epic of the modern Western consciousness as "Isolatoes all": that is, each has his own reason for being cut off from the normal health of mind that reflects a sure bond with fellow human beings, with nature, with destiny. Each is alienated; each, an ego-man fallen 'out of the hands of God.' Ahab, the ego-maniac, would of course be in charge of such a crew.

Just below Captain Ahab is the first mate, Starbuck. Starbuck is the finest kind of American: shrewd and sound, industrious and skillful, practical and pious. He has the instinct of goodness, is moderately well educated, is courageous but not crazy. Why is Starbuck so helpless before Ahab? Why does Ahab's purpose so completely dominate both Starbuck, as the most advanced type of responsible, idealistic, good-hearted American, and the primitive harpooneers (the red man, Tashtego; the black, Daggoo; the brown, Queequeg; even the "tawny," Fedallah)? The answer in the case of the harpooneers is simply that they do not participate in the structure of authority. In the case of Starbuck, however, the answer is that his "mere unaided virtue or right-mindedness" is but a relic or residue of Christian morality as passed down through ever more secular generations, in ever more attenuated and anemic form. Starbuck's state of virtue is no match for the Luciferic-Ahrimanic drive of demonic Ahab.

> Here, then, was this grey-headed, ungodly old man, chasing with curses a Job's whale round the world, at the head of a crew, too, chiefly made up of mongrel renegades, and cast-aways, and cannibals—morally enfeebled also, by the incompetence of mere unaided virtue or right-mindedness in Starbuck, the invulnerable jollity of indifference and recklessness in Stubb, and the pervading mediocrity in Flask. Such a crew, so officered, seemed specially picked and packed by some infernal fatality to help him to his monomaniac revenge. How it was that they so aboundingly responded to the old man's ire—by what evil magic their souls were possessed . . .—all this to explain, would be to dive deeper than Ishmael can go. (186)

Let us suppose that the reason the whole ship's company could be swept along by Ahab, regarding his mad quest as their own, is that all are partly moved by the spiritual principle that threatens to capture our own time; and that Ahab centrally *represents* this same spirit. How shall we identify the quality of being and striving that dominates Western civilization, that carries all before it, regardless of the fears or preferences that may at times make some of the passengers want to jump ship? Is it not a predatory pride of intellect that is bent upon harnessing and exploiting nature through the instrumentality of an ever more godless science and an ever more rapacious technology? When science becomes all brain and will, leaving out the heart; when it no longer allows itself to be taught by art or religion; when the scientific training of intelligence asks for no corresponding progress in moral and human development: then an Ahab mentality rules. Then Ahriman, behind Ahab, is in charge.

> So in dreams, have I seen majestic Satan thrusting forth his tormented, colossal claw from the flame Baltic of Hell. (376)

"Pure intellect," said Emerson, "is the pure devil." Contemptuously, the godless intellect extends its sway, bringing all into subjection. Captain Ahab, compassion squeezed from his heart under the pressure of urgencies and adversities he had called upon himself, became all intellect. He abandoned his human conscience towards his wife and child at home, towards his crew, towards the legitimate goals of his whaling voyage. He found himself offended by even the scientific quadrant, inasmuch as this represented to him the aspect of earthly science that still needs to take its bearings from heaven: "I trample on thee, thou paltry thing that feebly pointest on high; thus I split and destroy thee!" (494) The harpoon he fashioned for Moby Dick was quenched in human blood, and baptized in the name of the devil: *"Ego non baptizo te in nomine patris, sed in nomine diaboli!"* (484)

There can be no question but that cold-blooded technical thinking, pure abstract brainwork, aspires to become captain of the modern ship of state, especially in the West. Quite generally, those who excel in this kind of thinking are accorded elite status, both in and after their schooling. They tend to be proud, and to be aggressive. Though often they are not yet the leaders, quite as often the leaders must look to them for guidance. Blind to qualitative values, they tend to be impatient of the rights of individuals and to trample on the rights of nature.

Through Ahab, as the lurid image of the embattled technocrat cast larger than life on the screen of the future, Melville shows us how "That certain sultanism of his brain . . . became incarnate in an irresistible dictatorship." (144) It is not far-fetched to believe that the practical, prophetic instinct in Melville discerned over a hundred years ago how swiftly the modern world is moving towards dictatorship, an unprecedented dictatorship not only over the externalities of life but over the private mind and will as well. The artists, ministers, teachers, scientists, businessmen, statesmen of the last century have proven quite unable to halt this fatal trend. At their best, they are Starbucks: "morally enfeebled" in their "mere unaided virtue and right-mindedness."

The key words here, of course, are "mere unaided." In our time, what is unaided becomes mere. Ahab is filled alternately with the inhuman, anti-human impulses of Lucifer and Ahriman. He is thereby robbed of his free identity and all hope for human love or happiness; but his power is not mere. It is aided in the sense that superhuman agents work through him. *Moby Dick* was prophetic in showing that times were coming when men must once again reckon with the supernatural. The battle of good against evil is becoming ever more explicit; and those who wish to fight on the side of the good must want, and seek, and learn to receive, help—in a modern way—from the living spirit of goodness. To use the appropriate mythic analogy, those who would fight Leviathan, the dragon power, should pray for inspiration and courage from Marduk-Michael, wielder of the sacred sword and spear.

VIII

Melville has told us that he dreaded lest his story be taken for "a monstrous fable, or still worse and more detestable, a hideous and intolerable allegory." (204) Allegories are arbitrary intellectual constructions, and Melville knew that what he had to say was controlled by an instinct for truth that lay deeper than intellect can dive. He knew it was not a fancied fable but a true myth that was working itself out in his imagination, and that it unfolded according to a necessity rooted in the very nature of things. He embellished it from time to time, from this aspect and that, with such comments as might serve to hint its depths; but he did not presume to give it any final interpretation, for he sensed that the meaning of the whale went beyond Ahab's personal destiny. The overtones and undertones of the myth that inspired him sounded, like those of every true symbol, on many levels, cosmic as well as human. The riddle of mankind's relationship to the cosmic whale, after all, is at least as old and as enigmatic as the story of Jonah, which Melville made the prelude to his own rendering.

What was there about Jonah's whale that made him the symbol of all that meant most to the early Christians? He was, of course, the greatest of 'fishes'; but why in any case did a fish become the symbol of Christ? The Greek name for fish is *ichthys*, the first syllable of which, *ich*, in the German tongue means 'I,' the ego. These same three letters are also the initials of the name given to the Son of Man. But surely these first Christians were not merely playing with language when they made themselves secretly known to each other by tracing in the sand the figure of a fish.

Perhaps it is not far-fetched to think of the greatest fish as the earth itself: the earth Christ came to redeem, and with which he united himself. The earth swims and browses through the cosmic ether-ocean, yet it is the dwelling place of the human community. We men, whose origin is on high, find ourselves consigned to the earth for a term, for its sake and our own. To be swallowed up, as it were, into this whale's belly leaves us either so bewildered, frightened, and misled as to forget our origin altogether; or it provokes us mightily to remember and realize it. Out of the fish's belly, we pray with Jonah:

> out of the belly of hell cried I, and thou heardest my voice. For thou hadst cast me into the deep, in the midst of the seas; and the floods compassed me about; all thy billows and thy waves passed over me.
>
> Then I said, I am cast out of thy sight; yet I will look again toward thy holy temple.
>
> The waters compassed me about, even to the soul: the depth closed me round about, the weeds were wrapped about my head. I went down to the bottoms of the mountains; the earth with her bars was about me forever: yet hast thou brought up my life from corruption, O Lord my God.

The whale can carry us down and down, or it can rise with us to deliver us safely. The early Christians, who were themselves forced to live below ground in the catacombs, inscribed on their walls the sign of Jonah. Were they remembering that Christ, after his crucifixion, descended into the underworld for three days—the same length of time that Jonah spent in the whale's belly—in order to bring his redemption into the earth itself? Did it seem to them that the meaning of history lies in the choice mankind faces: to live its life on earth with or without Christ? Did they believe that the free choice of mankind would one day permit Christ to achieve what

Jonah, as representative of the still unaided human ego, could only augur but not complete: namely, the upward transformation, the spiritualization, of the great earth-whale?

Following the implications of this possibility, we come to see in the whale the symbol of earth's mighty abundance: its beauty, its strength, and its danger. We imagine that when mankind—every individual of it a Jonah—remains true to that light within itself which comes from beyond the earth, the living earth rejoices. Its creatures and energies become ever more harmonious and mutually helpful. But when men forget the light, the earth-experience darkens for all creatures as for man: that is, the whale dives to blackest depths.

Ahab, in the earlier form of his egoism, had coveted to possess rather than to serve the light. Frustrated in his assault upon the heights, he became bitter, even as Jonah in his spiritual pride had done. Of Jonah it was said that he was exceedingly displeased and very angry with the Lord for the way He had managed things. And when the Lord asked him, "Doest thou well to be angry?" Jonah replied, "I do well to be angry, even unto death." While Jonah, however, became suicidal in simply deciding to withdraw from life, Ahab's suicidal impulse took the form of a violent attack. When Lucifer had not brought him the heavenly victory he sought, he abandoned himself to Ahriman's power, in the vain hope to gain at least an earthly triumph of vengeance. Torn between Lucifer and Ahriman, and spurning the hint of salvation held out to him through the humble simplicity of Pip, Ahab could not find the true victor, the true friend of mankind and of the earth. His second error inevitably proved as disastrous as his first.

IX

Through the voyage of the *Pequod* Melville shows what happens when mankind as a whole sets out under the command of a ruthless intelligence and an arrogant will, to dominate and exploit the earth that was given it for quite another purpose. The *Pequod* set itself to hunt down the creature who, as we have suggested, of all beings on earth best symbolizes the innocence and abundance of nature's spiritual energy. The hunting, killing, stripping and boiling down with its own fire, of the ever-diminishing whale population, is as exact a picture as one could find for the main task so-called productive—actually consuming—modern civilizations set before themselves. Once upon a time there were many whales and few whalers, even as in the Arctic there have always been many caribou and some wolves. A symbiotic relationship favorable to both sides could possibly be maintained. But as men grow smart, bold, greedy and uncaring, they invent technical improvements to kill whales faster, with less effort. The whales grow scarcer; the hunt intensifies. Technology now dominates the operation of whaling. The whole fishery can no longer be seen as man working in and with nature; certainly not as man for nature but clearly as man against nature, with no holds barred.

> Now, then, thought I . . . here goes for a cool, collected dive at death and destruction, and the devil fetch the hindmost. (228)

In the mirror that life itself holds up to man, we see technological civilization—which is to say, many aspects of modern America as exemplified in the ship *Pequod* under Captain Ahab—advancing against the living earth in a predatory, merciless, coldly cruel manner. The image that advances therefore from within the mirror, the incalculably vicious whale, symbolizes the changed aspect of nature as henceforth she may be expected to present herself. As attackers, we are met by the picture of nature malignant, nature gone berserk.

If one wonders how such a phenomenon could happen, he should ask those who study weather, nutrition, public health, and ecology. He should observe that loss of fertility follows the over-use of chemical fertilizers; that as fruits and vegetables are brought to greater external perfection they lose in nutritive value; that intensive use of pesticides and antibiotics results in more virulent pests and disease organisms; that triumphs of irrigation result in salinization of the earth and lowered water tables. He should note that the victories over infectious disease of which we are so proud, are accompanied by an increase of all types of degenerative disease: cardiac, muscular, skeletal, glandular, nervous. He should consider, in other words, what may be called the legion paradoxes of technical 'progress.'

A civilization that prefers quantity to quality, substance to form, may expect to meet its nemesis in cancerous overgrowths of all kinds: whether of bodily tissues, of population, of government, of cities, of corporations, of automobiles, or of money. A civilization that honors only matter will be overwhelmed by its own refuse and pollution. Believing only in the physical senses, it will fall prey to eroticism, gluttony and the like. Excessively mental, it will wear itself out in the race to be as instantaneous as thought. Growing all to head, it will have no way to escape the fatal deposits of chalk in artery and joint. A civilization built upon a coldly technical attitude that seeks many kinds of testimony but never that of the heart, will be struck down typically by heart failure.

America suffers acutely from all of these paradoxes, and we know that in particular it is one of the most unhealthful nations in the world precisely for the human heart. In Melville it found a prophet whose own constitution prepared him to speak from and for the man of heart and lungs. "I stand for the heart," he wrote.* Anyone may convince himself of Melville's preoccupation with the mysteries of the heart who will take the trouble to count the quite extraordinary number of times in such books as *Moby Dick* and *Pierre*—on practically every page, in many sections—Melville refers to the heart and lungs, to the chest. Whether his outlook on life determined this focus, or this constitutional focus determined his outlook, Melville's genius is connected with the heart—with the failed heart. And questions of heart, taking heart in its highest symbolic meaning as well as physically, are the issue for America.

The heart strives ever to equilibrate and harmonize what occurs above in the cerebral-cognitional man with what occurs below in the visceral-volitional man. Even so, Melville, a prophetic representative of America itself, lived always as one torn between these two worlds; his greatness came to deep intuitions of both, but did not suffice to reconcile them. He perceived how man's experience of the world alternates, as the heart itself beats, between form and force, coldness and warmth, death and life; but he could not discover how to convert this perpetual conflict between opposites into a loving collaboration in which thinking and doing, self and world, heaven and earth, idealism and realism might find a

* From a letter to Nathaniel Hawthorne in the spring of 1851, quoted on p. 109 in *Herman Melville, Cycle and Epicycle*, by Eleanor Melville Metcalf. (Cambridge, Harvard University Press, 1953.)

collaborative, creative outlet in unequivocal wisdom, in well-tempered happiness, and in the sure mastery of circumstances. His difficulty in achieving this solution made Melville all the more a specialist in the problems that concern the heart. It enabled him to foretell most forcefully what must happen to a people who advance in both intellectuality and power, but who fail to develop the heart to master them.

It is well known that in the end Ahab loses his life to the whale, who also rams and sinks the *Pequod.* We are led to see that if it comes to a showdown, cosmic nature will surely humble man's willfulness. Nature will rebel; man's predatory arrogance will find itself crushed by a greater power that only man himself makes relentless. But the precise picture that Melville gives us of this last event is worth remembering. As the stove ship subsides into the remorseless sea, her three masts are still for a moment visible, topped by the three pagan harpooneers. As we watch the American Indian, Tashtego, strike a last blow to nail Ahab's torn flag back to the top of the mainmast, we see a swooping, intercepting sky-hawk—"the bird of heaven" who may be the Pacific Ocean's nearest representative of the American eagle—caught beneath the hammer and carried down with the ship. The prophecy is fatal, but only for an America that would allow itself to be commandeered all the way into the future by a mentality that values power above love.

BIBLIOGRAPHY

Emerson, Ralph Waldo. *The Selected Writings of Ralph Waldo Emerson.* New York, Modern Library, Random House, 1950.

Melville, Herman. *Moby Dick*. New York, Modern Library, Random House, 1950.

Thoreau, Henry David. *Walden and Other Writings of Henry David Thoreau*, Ed. Brooks Atkinson. New York, Modern Library, Random House, 1950.

Whitman, Walt. *The Portable Walt Whitman.* Ed. Mark Van Doren. New York, Viking Press, 1945.

Publications Available from The Myrin Institute
521 Park Avenue, New York, New York 10021

Books

	Hard Cover	Soft Cover
The Experience of Knowledge by John F. Gardner	$8.95	$4.50
Man: The Bridge Between Two Worlds by Franz E. Winkler	—	$4.50
For Freedom Destined: Mysteries of Man's Evolution in the Mythology of Wagner's Ring Operas and Parsifal by Franz E. Winkler	$6.95	$3.95
Can the Red Man Help the White Man? ed. by Sylvester M. Morey	—	$1.95
Respect for Life: The Traditional Upbringing of American Indian Children ed. by Sylvester M. Morey and Olivia L. Gilliam	—	$3.50
The Recovery of Man in Childhood by A. C. Harwood	—	$4.95

Proceedings

No. 1 Seminar on Comparative Education: Islamic Values in Education & The Liberal Arts Tradition

No. 2 The Influence of Psychology on Education
by Franz E. Winkler

No. 3 The Scientific Spirit of Inquiry*
by Russell W. Davenport

No. 4 Portrait of a Waldorf School
by A. C. Harwood

No. 5 Man's Mathematical Mind: from Thales to Wiener
by John Kreitner

No. 6 The Scientific and the Moral in Education
by L. Francis Edmunds

No. 7 The American College: A Proposal for Reform
by Russell Kirk

No. 7a National Psychology in International Relations
by Franz E. Winkler

No. 8 The Psychology of Leadership
by Franz E. Winkler

No. 9 The Cleavage between Intellectual and Spiritual Life
by Robert Ulich

The Battle That Was Not Fought
by Franz E. Winkler

No. 10 The Map of Childhood
by A. C. Harwood
(Now available only in the book, The Recovery of Man in Childhood. See above.)

No. 11 Man: The Bridge Between Two Worlds (A chapter from . . .)
by Franz E. Winkler
(Now available only in the book, Man: The Bridge Between Two Worlds. See above.)

No. 12 Reflections on Discipline
by John F. Gardner

No. 13 American Indians and Our Way of Life
by Sylvester M. Morey

No. 14 The Experience of Knowledge
by John F. Gardner

No. 15 Intuition, Intellect and the Racial Question
by Laurens van der Post

No. 16 The Mythology in Wagner's "Rhinegold"
by Franz E. Winkler
(Now available only in the book, For Freedom Destined. See above.)

No. 17 America in Foreign Affairs
by Cornelis H. DeJong

No. 18 Towards a Truly Public Education
by John F. Gardner

No. 19 The Mythology in Wagner's "Valkyrie" and "Siegfried"
by Franz E. Winkler

No. 20 The Mythology in Wagner's "Twilight of the Gods"
by Franz E. Winkler

No. 21 The Mythology in Wagner's "Parsifal"
by Franz E. Winkler

No. 22 Right Action, Right Thinking
by John F. Gardner

No. 23 One's Man Vision: In Memoriam, H. A. W. Myrin

No. 24 The Secret of Peace and The Environmental Crisis
by John F. Gardner

No. 25 The Role of Technology in the Modern World
by Frederick J. Kreitner

No. 26 Love and the Illusion of Love
by John F. Gardner

No. 27 The Blind in Society and Blindness, A New Seeing of the World
by Jacques Lusseyran

No. 28 The Idea of Man in America
by John F. Gardner

No. 29 Marihuana Today
by George K. Russell

No. 30 Against the Pollution of the I
by Jacques Lusseyran

No. 31 The Poverty of a Rich Society
by John F. Gardner

No. 32 Melville's Vision of America
by John F. Gardner

*Currently out of print

Proceedings Numbers 1-31 are sold in bookstores for $1 per copy, Numbers 32 and up for $1.50 per copy, and are available directly from the Myrin Institute for a suggested contribution of $1 or more to cover the cost of printing and mailing.

Pamphlets

About Marijuana by Franz E. Winkler	$ .30
What Is An Alcoholic? by George W. McCarthy	$ .30
Vivisection and the True Aims of Education in Biology by George K. Russell	$ .50

Contributions Welcomed

The Myrin Institute is supported by voluntary contributions. If you are interested in its work and care to make a gift, large or small, it will be gratefully received. Contributions are tax-deductible.

Write: The Myrin Institute, 521 Park Avenue, New York, New York 10021.